T0274748

Archives
of Joy

Reflections on Animals
and the Nature of Being

Jean-François Beauchemin
TRANSLATED BY DAVID WARRINER

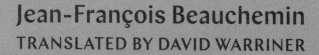

Archives of
JOY

GREYSTONE BOOKS
Vancouver/Berkeley/London

First published in English by Greystone Books in 2023
Originally published in French as *Archives de la joie: Petit traité
de métaphysique animale*, copyright © 2018 by Les Éditions
Québec Amérique inc., Montréal, Québec. All rights reserved.
English translation copyright © 2023 by David Warriner

23 24 25 26 27   5 4 3 2 1

Greystone Books Ltd.
greystonebooks.com

Cataloguing data available from Library and Archives Canada
ISBN 978-1-77164-932-2 (cloth)
ISBN 978-1-77164-933-9 (epub)

Editing for original edition by Marie-Noëlle Gagnon,
Sylvie Martin, and Sabrina Raymond
Copy editing by Paula Ayer
Proofreading by Alison Strobel
Cover and text design by Jessica Sullivan
Cover and interior illustrations © Annie Konst via Creative Market

Printed and bound in Canada on FSC® certified paper at Friesens. The FSC®
label means that materials used for the product have been responsibly sourced.

Greystone Books thanks the Canada Council for the Arts, the
British Columbia Arts Council, the Province of British Columbia
through the Book Publishing Tax Credit, and the Government
of Canada for supporting our publishing activities.

Greystone Books gratefully acknowledges the xʷməθkʷəy̓əm (Musqueam),
Sḵwx̱wú7mesh (Squamish), and səlílwətaʔɬ (Tsleil-Waututh) peoples on
whose land our Vancouver head office is located.

When the bird rests, it knows
where to rest. Should a human
being be unequal to a bird?

CONFUCIUS

Contents

Author's Note

Every other day since the start of summer, an old deer with a grizzled gray snout has been wandering into my garden to dream away some of what little time he has left. The light around him pivots by a few degrees, arranging its photons as if to ready him for his passing into the beyond. As his body escapes him a little more each day, I think that he's slowly coming around to a more abstract and somehow purer way of seeing the world. It's as if his subconscious has fallen out of sync with him and the intricacies and intensity of his life in the forest. From the look in his eye, and the story of sorts that it seems to tell, one remarkably real thing emerges: joy. I know that joy. It's the same joy I feel every time that I, like my old grizzled deer, turn around and notice the few great, steadfast constructions of my past. It's been during times like these, as I've reflected on these things, and on that joy, that I've written this book. This is not a novel, nor is it a collection of poetry. It is not an essay, a diary, or a work of autofiction. Rather, as animals feature so prominently, I like to think of this as a bestiary of memory. We should stop saying that it's not good to look back, that we must keep forging ahead and looking forward—always forward. I'm going to come right out and say it: I felt instantly happier when I began to embrace, appreciate, and constantly revisit my past. I'm not trying to say the future has nothing going for it. I saw myself there just the other day and it wasn't bad; I still had my gentle fury and my methodical sense of secrecy, my snowmanly solitude, and my pain-streaked wonderment. But my interest in what I observe in the past is growing, and arguably this is precisely because I believe I can see the future taking shape in there, trying to find its way, choosing which of my actions have the greatest chance of panning out. Ultimately, that's the story these pages tell. It's not the story of a (really quite ordinary) life, but rather a trajectory—the curve of a moving object, a stone thrown at the windows of time and duration in an attempt to let something out. What, exactly? A certain, forgotten way of seeing the world, perhaps? I wonder if that is what these animals have been hankering for me to remember.

J.-F. B.

In the Forest

It was one of the last evenings in August and summer had well and truly vacated. That day, I had exhausted what little of my childhood remained in reserve. My heart was a big spiral staircase that didn't know if it was going up or down. As I always do when I'm trying to find my footing, I went to stroll a few steps in the forest. Around seven o'clock, as the light was beginning to fade, I saw two deer spring out and bound away into the trees. Of course, Camus set off in pursuit, and I lost sight of him for several long minutes. Then I called him, and the dog came scampering back, snapping dead branches in his wake, shattering the almost supernatural silence of these woods. There was an expression of pure joy sparkling in his eyes. Panting for breath, he lay down in the dirt and refused to keep walking with me. So, I stayed by his side until he had gathered his strength. Night was falling. We were in a clearing, and the sky over our heads was shifting imperceptibly. For a while I listened to the tinkling crystal of the shifting stars, then it all accelerated and in barely a half hour, a constellation that had risen earlier in the west climbed to the north, trailing behind it the slim crescent moon

I had seen from my window the night before. I let my mind wander a little and said to myself for the thousandth time that I wasn't cut out for real life. Then an owl hooted its piercing, lonely cry. The dog suddenly pricked his ears with alertness and flashed me a look of sheer surprise. The urge to light a fire came to me right there and then, but I knew Manon, back at the house, would be worried if we stayed out too late. So I suggested to Camus that we head back, to which he consented only after a long and impenetrable moment of reflection.

Splash

The light was beautiful, casting across the pond the infinite glints of its jewels. I brought the rowboat to a halt near the big rock that sticks out from the water and spent a half hour observing the tortoise basking—or daydreaming—there, her little head tilted toward the sun. Perhaps she was secretly musing about Harriet, the famous Galápagos giant tortoise who lived a hundred and seventy-five years, or Adwaita, whose venerable age of two-hundred-and-fifty-plus years commanded respect among his fellow residents at the zoo in the city formerly known as Calcutta. I find it quite bothersome that you can't utter the word *death* without passing for a killjoy, but still, I rather had the impression that it was precisely upon her death that the tortoise in the little pond was reflecting at that moment. I was rejoicing at the idea that I was perhaps not alone in entertaining such a thought even in the full light of day, at the height of summer, and while the living is altogether so easy. Thankfully I am not a troubled soul, nor am I sad or annoyed with my life; I am simply a man who is always moved and amazed by the brevity of everything, and who strives to at least balance this brevity a little by way of the counterweights within my reach, be it joy, for instance, or otherwise the seeking of beauty. And I am not always fond of my habit of expressing things in the way of a man who turns a deaf ear, but I am yet to find any other way to say that, of all my thoughts, that of my death remains the most difficult to make heard. In any case, I wondered whether she too, my tortoise, had the feeling of a big spiky flowering cactus growing at her life's center. The subtle *splash* her body made in the water in parting gave nothing away.

The Soul

————

Through the entire summer of 1959, that is to say, the time when I was not even in Mother's belly yet, every day I went out at dawn into the countryside, stick in hand, in search of my soul. I would never meet anyone but I would hear, coming from some distant path, the always somewhat hoarse voice of a news-crier, and from farther away still, the muffled purring of farm machines. My heart of course was not yet beating, but there waiting, in the middle of my chest, was a small and quite joyful yellow bird, who had flown from the sun down a broad stream of warmth. All day long, I would observe the sky passing right by, returning, adjusting its course, to eventually hang over the derelict customs officers' barrier. Often in the evening I would light a fire and amuse myself by imagining my brothers keeping watch on the landing for my arrival, with their crewcut hair, buttonhole suspenders, and patent-leather shoes, and perhaps with a flea-bitten cat or dog by their side too. Then, once I had weighed up good and proper the pros and cons of this coming life, I would return home to the dog-eared book, read and reread, recounting the meeting of my father and mother. On the way back, I would notice as always, on the crest of the hill, the faint glimmer of a still-open inn, then that of a barn where farm animals watched over one another. Later I would fall asleep thinking about the time and the place where I would be born, and I would remember that in order to subsist every human community needs a set of values that transcends the individuals and gives meaning to their collective existence. And since this world I was preparing to enter wasn't going in that direction, I would muse that I, and others, would have to find a way to encourage the sense of the sacred (but good grief, not the religious), to foster a kind of civic thinking firmly grounded in Human Rights, of course, but also embellished by secular laws, by schools, and in particular by the lessons of History. That was how I used to while away my days, at the time.

Dreamer

I recently spent several hours consoling Rêveur, a grand old dreamer of a horse whose long working life on the farm was coming to an end. I spoke to him as naturally as possible. He responded by snorting a thick cloud of vapor out of his nostrils. For him, his imminent death did not seem to be the worst of concessions. He had very much enjoyed pulling the cart, but I understood that the decline in time devoted to his dreams was his heaviest loss. For sadly, he now slept little (three hours a day on average), and less and less while standing, preferring to lay his great emaciated body down so the cycles of REM sleep, the sole gateways to his reverie, would open. At this solemn hour of his life, no thoughts of the hereafter haunted his mind, and in his gaze framed by long lashes of horsehair I could see that he found my brain and its way of making the absolute from the approximate and the incomplete rather amusing. By his way of sometimes stopping and opening his eyes wide, one might think that memory, for him, was a deep well and that he was amazed by its contents once the bucket was hauled up. Like all mammals, he was the nostalgic type. He might have been reminiscing,

I suppose, about that great, impossible love for a mare twice his age, whose rump sat so fitted in the harness it put him all in a fluster. I walked by his side in the tall grass, beneath the fine blue structures of the sky. We saw birds of passage flying westward, filling their eyes with images aplenty. It was July of 2017; fifty-seven years had flown by since my birth, and twenty-nine since his, over there, in the little stable strewn with hay. I brought my step in time with his, the step of an old herbivore aware that with his death a wealth of gathered knowledge and affection given and received would disappear. I marveled at the similarities of our respective existences and the fact that the days, all in all, had stacked up one after the other like the pages of a book, in which over time the words had changed but what had inspired them still remained. Essentially, he and I had been just two beings moving away from a childhood that never tired of catching up with them.

A Visitor

The day I turned eight (July 13, 1968), a car from a far-away place drove into our street, gleaming in the fiery glow of morning. It drew up in front of the house, and out stepped its sole occupant. He closed the door without a sound and moved ever so gently toward me—I who had just spent the night in tears because the previous day I had learned my dog's life expectancy was only fourteen years. "Good morning, I am God," he said to me quite simply, albeit in a seraphic tone. "Would you allow me to sit for a moment?" Then he sat down beside me on the old bench, and after a brief silence he started to ramble about everything and nothing. I sensed that he was not there to express his thoughts clearly per se, but rather to suggest something, as in the poems of Stéphane Mallarmé or André Breton, which I would sometimes read. I did not dare point it out, but for goodness' sake, I thought, if I were God, I would engage people in a prodigiously deep and intelligible conversation abounding with meticulous wonder and meditative precision. Anyhow, we conversed in this manner for a while, him going on with his still somewhat vague words, as if he didn't really know what to say, and me with mine, secular and grieving. After a half hour or so he rose, bid me a very polite farewell, returned to his car, started the engine, did a U-turn, and disappeared around the street corner. I never saw him again. All my life I've reflected on that brief encounter. Today I think that, deep down inside, he must have realized some time beforehand that he had made a mistake by granting dogs such a short life expectancy, and wanted to come apologize in person for such an outrageous error in planning.

A Writer's Life

At the time I was still just a young, inexperienced writer, but thankfully I had instincts, which always come in handy until knowledge, or habit, can sort through one's ideas and actions. Everything in my first books had been written without resorting much to devices of reasoning, nor to explicit adjustments of technique. Still, one of those books (*Garage Molinari*) was such a success that it alone enabled me to finish paying for my house and start planning for the land-scaping of the garden. In April I bought several young trees, the planting and care of which kept me occupied all summer long. Because they made me think about certain pursuits of the mind (digging, rooting, seeking light, nourishing, and weeding, for instance), these horticultural activities inspired me, and my handling of times to come. Every week or almost, television, radio, or the newspapers would call me, and so in the company of some highly conscientious interviewers I would try to unravel the mystery of my rather unex-pected success. Neither they nor I ever did a very good job. Afterward, I would go home, push open the little spring-loaded gate parting the potentilla hedge in two, and enter the garden. I would then inspect my trees one last time, and sit down in the shade to reread *Garage Molinari*. No, I could not quite understand how I had managed to write such a tender, funny, and tragic book. But nor could I understand how my trees managed to grow, nor how one day such astonishing fruits would appear at the ends of their branches. It pained me to let people believe I had an enigmatic mind. A writer's life, like a writer's thoughts, is never very complicated. You get up early, you feed the dog and the cat, and then you pull on your big boots and go out to water the garden. These tasks accomplished, you stay awhile to observe the sky turning on its axis, a giant traffic circle in the air, the birds merging one by one into the flow. Then, you go upstairs to write a few sentences, a page if all goes well, and like every day you find yourself nonplussed at having to observe a certain, curiously indispensable silence before the words come. Barely any time later, you're thinking about random things again, like that time during your childhood when you would always turn your bed to follow the position of the Pole Star, because you had a vague sense that your destiny was connected to that star. Then the dog appears in the doorway with his leash in his mouth, and that's when you know your working day is over.

Announcement

One morning in June last year, four deer came into our garden. The one who seemed to be the leader approached so closely, I got to hold his snout in my hand for a moment. During that time, the three others stood back, constantly casting glances left and right, like the bodyguards of a president on a foreign mission. Then they all ambled slowly away and returned to the forest. Two days later, I saw them come back, this time with a little one who had clearly been born mere hours earlier. Very often I think about these messengers who came to me to announce the birth of one of their own. I have no theory to explain the sense of closeness and connection I have felt to deer since that time. Perhaps I am so drawn to them because they defy all explanation. I am continually moved by these timid beings, steeped in wary, woodsy contemplation, graced with a playful spring in their step and a synchrony of memory. I am quite sure that their mind's eye holds an everlasting, airy daydream of a big red sun with people whirling about in their finest new clothes and a cascade of colors, just like a Marc Chagall painting. Alas, I only have intermittent access to this metaphorical world. I try my best to stay awhile, but all I can manage are fleeting moments. The images in my memory and imagination are not terribly compatible with those I think I see swirling in the gaze of my elusive visitors. The wood-wormed doors, half-moored rowboats, and secret infernos of my mind will always be foreign to the concerns of these beautiful animals. Still, they and I walk in step, and at night we lift our gaze to the same stars.

Running

I used to listen to conversations and hear people everywhere saying that death always caught up with us
in the end. That was why I spent a good part of my
childhood trying to outrun it—by taking up running.
What's more, at school I ended up winning races, and
even getting medals for running, which earned me
my very first kiss as I stepped down from the podium.
Suzie Aleystock was eleven years old, an alluring Black
girl with impossibly blue eyes who liked my type,
that is to say, guys who were athletic, socially inept,
and academically challenged, though not for a lack of
studying. We dated that entire school year and formed
quite the prominent couple, racking up the accolades.
Sue was so popular, she was unanimously crowned
Miss Constellation 1972. The stardom reflected on me
as well and I found myself basking in her glow like
some kind of rock star, in miniature. Still, I kept on
running like a maniac. Every day people would see me
galloping in the streets, sprinting anywhere I had to be,
dashing to the park or the corner store whenever my
mother sent me out to buy milk, running here, there,

and everywhere until I was out of breath. The dogs in the neighborhood would watch me go by in bewilderment. Now I don't believe for a second that these creatures are inferior beings, unworthy of our altruism. What I observe each day is that, like us, they live a never wholly decipherable life—not as mystical as ours, but no less mysterious. But back then I always resisted the temptation to stop, stroke their head, and connect with them, as I have since done so much. I would run, and run. People would nickname me The Sprinter, or The Ostrich. They would marvel at the firmness of my calves and the striking aerodynamics of my hamstrings. But no one would remark that with almost every stride, I would cast an eye over my shoulder to see whether or not death was catching up with me.

Before I Was Born

Before I was born, I endeavored to do things out of love, knowing that I would soon have to do them mainly out of necessity. For instance, even though there was really no need, I would sing nearly all the time, especially on days when my mind was having a sudden growth spurt. The presence of a dog, or perhaps a cow, was all that I was missing back then. That way, I could have shared some impressions with either of them, examined the repercussions of the coming birth. Of course, our interactions would still have been those of a human and an animal, but that would not have prevented us from exploring a great many subjects and topical issues together. Often, at that stage of my life, the sky turning on its hinges would sound like the turning of pages. It seems quite clear to me that my taste for books and for reading dates back to that time and to those hours spent scrutinizing that wrinkling of paper sheets in the sky. There were no calendars in Mother's belly, but I would count on my fingers the days separating me from my arrival at home, from this post-aquatic life filled with strength and joy. It eventually happened around

nine in the morning on July 13, 1960, before the awe-
struck eyes of my father in his shirtsleeves, so moved
that he forgot to take off his hat. Three days after my
birth I noticed my sister for the first time, whom people everywhere said was a tomboy. On the contrary, I
immediately found that she was a highly accomplished
girl, far more intelligent than those of us males in our
still incomplete but already promise-filled family. It
was she in particular who taught me, around the age
of six, the meaning of sharing and redistribution of
wealth (intellectual, moral, temporal, material, and
emotional) since as everyone knows, in the small world
where children live, nothing is more intensely felt than
injustice. In short, I could barely believe I had just been
born; since the beginning I'd had the sense of being
craftier than the void from whence I had come, of having stripped it of something, some sort of prebiotic joy
from a world before the real. What I'm trying to say is
that a phenomenon I can't yet explain very well led me
to be born old and start at the end, and to take a very
early interest in what old age had in store for me. It's
a wonderful thing, because now that I'm almost two-
thirds of the way through my life, age is behind me
and I can feel my youth setting in. Before I was born,
as well, I would spend an hour a day observing a fine
portrait of my parents. I remember my father with his

newspaper and his old camera with the magnesium flash, and Mother's face as she once more reread the letter that had come in the mail that morning. Sometimes I would think I heard someone knocking softly at the door and say to myself, "That must be Manon," but I would forget that we were not supposed to meet until the age of twenty-eight, after a fair few heartaches, several cars towed to the pound, and plenty of pints drunk. At times I would receive a visit from a man unknown to me but so attentive to my words he could see my future. Already he knew that I was going to be an artist, that my needs would only be modest, and that there would almost always be the friendly nuzzling of a dog to complement my strolls. He said, too, that despite the truth being sad I would never stop seeking it. That I would not be the most serious of men but would willingly take interest in serious matters. That every pain caused by me would never be by calculation but rather emanate from a kind of bare, untamed solitude. That I would never get used to my life. That all in all I would accomplish very few truly useful things.

Useful

I don't yet know where the limits of the physical world end. For instance, quite often, the essence of my thinking escapes me and disperses in the body as if this were what it was nourishing, and not the mind. Books have helped me greatly to define these limits more clearly. At any rate, I have drawn inspiration from reading about nuthatches, little birds who in one season can stow away as many as three hundred thousand seeds—tens of times more than they will ever need. It might be said that I am rummaging around a lot in that great big suitcase of my childhood, but why the devil do we age, if it is not to encounter ourselves once more? Nevertheless, to this day reading instills a sense of calm quite like that which washed over me when, at the age of eleven, I helped a cow to give birth. When that brave creature leaned into my body for me to comfort her from all her pain, I felt extremely useful in this world.

Happy People

The peaceful home of our neighbors, Mr. and Mrs. Chung, sits among the trees some distance away from ours. Some summer nights, when the weather is mild and the trill of the chorus frogs is sounding down by the pond, Mr. and Mrs. Chung come out onto their patio with their two daughters, and all four of them sing songs from their faraway Korean homeland. A startling melancholy takes hold of the surrounding environment. In the forest, the animals pause their usual activities for a moment and prick up their ears. The moon, thus far climbing skyward, hangs still among the branches. Even our cat, who usually seeks contact with things so keenly, looks out, barely touching a thing, at this fragile, ephemeral world. Later, once the voices of Mr. and Mrs. Chung and their daughters have fallen silent, we thread our way through the trees to their house with our kettle and share a steaming pot of tea with them. I've always enjoyed the company of happy people. I feel that by being with them, I'm increasing my chances of being contaminated by their happiness. It's not as stupid as it seems. Being beside happiness is obviously not the same thing as being happy, but it makes me think of my father-in-law, who was a printer. "What is an imprint?" he would often muse philosophically, wiping his ink-stained fingers on his rustic old shirt. "An imprint is the impression left on an object by the pressure of another object, whatever that may be." Of course, it would be quite simplistic to equate the movements of the human heart to the effects of a rotary press, but to this day I must admit that a considerable part of my happiness rests on the thought of an impression made on my life by that of others.

Adjectives

I used to have a very antisocial cat who liked no one but me, and who every six months or so would wander off to go live his life. Weeks would go by before he came home injured, horribly emaciated, and infested with fleas, albeit with a gaze of infinity and immemorial dreams. And so, the philosophical rapport that had always existed between us would be restored. In the morning, when I sat down to write, he would stretch out on my desk and take an interest in my sentences. It seemed to me that my pragmatic pages grated on his nerves, and that was why one day I began to place words here and there that perhaps added nothing to the general meaning, but that breathed little puffs of poetry into it, each one like a tiny lamp casting light on the surrounding paragraphs. By way of example, that was the time to which my habit of resorting to qualifying adjectives the likes of *metaphorical, molecular, indefatigable*, and *woodwormed* dates back. These are words that could generally be avoided, but whose mood-lighting services are very useful to me. Thanks to them, the atmosphere of my books is more inviting. Once, a critic invited me to speak on television, only to accuse me of abusing adjectives. I replied that I couldn't help it, that my cat was the one he should be saying that sort of thing to. The following year I published a new, rather realistic book in which it was clear the lighting was functional above all else. My critic liked it a lot, but I didn't care. I was thinking about my trusty old cat who some months earlier had gone off in search of other dreams and impassable horizons, perhaps also in search of a little poetry.

Carefree

—————

I was barely ten years old when, after saving dutifully, I pocketed the necessary three dollars, mounted my bicycle, and hastened to the farmer's, where the rabbit I had been thinking about for a month was waiting. The ride home was even shorter: I was impatient to initiate my new companion to domestic life. I loved that dreamer's spirit of his, those ears cocked to catch the slightest rumor, and the fine composure intelligible in those black-ringed eyes. I didn't share the same complicity with him as with my dog. All in all, I spoke to him quite little, because I figured my actions were sufficient for him to understand me. But in a glance he could sense my every hesitation, my every alarm, my every sorrow. I learned to live with his silences, some of which appeared to contain the answers my young intelligence could not yet find. We were both used to the same simple things, deprived of the supernatural, and yet fathomless. I was already an atheist at that time, but to increase my chances I would still pray to Jesus each day to protect him from the foxes and the clutches of the owls. But he didn't experience that kind of apprehension mixed with approximate catechism. His religion,

dare I say, was limited to a sort of vegetable-patch exis-
tentialism. For that matter, I think my hypersensitivity
moved him and inspired his respect. By way of example, in my presence he never sneaked under the fence to
munch the neighbor's heads of lettuce. His crimes were
only committed in my absence, or at night, while I was
sleeping and he would not risk disappointing me. To
broach the future, I used to turn over tarot cards on the
lawn in front of him. Three-quarters of the time they
were in his favor, which clearly comforted him. I thus
insisted a little less on introducing him to my soothing
Buddhist practices, but I did continue to consecrate my
Monday evenings in his company to sitting in Buddha's
cobra position. On other occasions, quivering a little,
shameful as a Catholic, I dared to tell him about all those
times when I had pretended to agree with grown-ups,
the way you do with fools to please them. Afterward, I
could sense that he was a little burdened by this, and so
I would run to the pantry and bring back more food for
him than usual. A contented smile of sorts would then
adorn his whiskered face. Since when one is happy, the
mind lets go of ballast.

Apollinaire

I was not, like my brothers and my sister, endowed with great genius, but I compensated for what I lacked in mind by observing and dreaming. I already had a lot of *idées fixes* (the contemplation of animals, the petrifying beauty of the sky, the hypnotic charm of books, et cetera) and I sensed that it was not without reason, that in a way these ideas were prophecies of the mature man who I was to become and who was waiting for me, hair all unkempt, right in the middle of my life. At night, hiding beneath the sheets, I used to turn on my flashlight and discover the ballistic power of adjectives in the dictionary. I was ten years old and my ambition was to earn my living writing poems inspired by those of Guillaume Apollinaire, whose heart-shaped calligram "Mon Cœur pareil à une flamme renversée"—my heart like an inverted flame—had become my motto. My perspective on poems has much changed since, but I continue to find pleasure in the company of the poets themselves, mostly because of the messy kinds of flowers blossoming in their souls. When you love life like I did, a good reserve of daydreams is a necessity. I used to watch my friends live their lives and find that they were old, that they lacked illusions. Only their actions shaped and defined them; it was as if they had renounced the inventive and subtle impetus of their great fetal period. Besides my brothers and my sister I was misunderstood by most people, though I didn't make a drama of it. My successes in society rested on something other than my historically so ill-adapted intellect. In retrospect, I see that these successes were solely due to the love I bestowed on all the creatures I encountered, which far later, for that matter, ended up forming the essence of my human work. In my moments of delirium, when for example I would inadvertently breathe the secondhand smoke from my brother Pierre's marijuana cigarettes, a mysterious piety would take hold of me. Some hours would pass, during which I believed in God and addressed him with a pensive kind of severity. But, as always, all it took was for me to read a few verses of Apollinaire for my life to return to order. One of my concerns was to preserve my peace of mind. I understood that my efforts had borne their fruit when I noticed that this maintained peace beautified my thinking. My body was modifying itself constantly, like a plant. On the whole I liked that period of my life, but at times I would find myself impatient to leave it and go see to what extent this body conceived from nothing would pursue its materialization, whether to this end it would continue to draw from the supply of my dreams. It's a long story to say a simple thing: to be a child would have been a wonder.

A House Sparrow

Once, for a whole summer, I looked after a house sparrow who, I am almost certain, had been banished from
his community for heresy. His feathered fellows, all
vegetarians, were wearing themselves out looking for
the seeds and grains of their daily menu. But every day
he came to feed in the simplest way in the world on the
bugs splattered on the car radiator. His contradictory
spirit had brilliantly led him to develop an attitude of
great skepticism. I found him quite in keeping with the
mindset of the philosopher Spinoza, whose doctrine
proposes a rationalist conduct free from any form of
Utopian idealism. When he had had his fill, I would see
him cast me a sideways glance, then hop a few times on
the hood before flying over to join me on the top tread
of the steps. For long minutes we would stay there on
the porch observing the other sparrows frantically
come and go, with empty stomachs, anxious for their
future. I remember, at that time I was more interested
than necessary in the person of Jesus and would read
over the New Testament with a highlighter. Like most
human beings I see everything very clearly at certain
times, and at others, on the contrary, reality seems

disproportionately foggy to me. I figured that if I had lived by his side, I would have asked Christ to be more explicit on certain important questions. For example, I would have suggested he tell people frankly that the idea of God may be comforting but is not indispensable. Above all, I would have urged him to clarify the notion of earthly life, with its duration so short it obliges us to surpass ourselves. One evening, around the firepit by the olive tree, I would have turned to one or another of his disciples (probably John, the youngest and most prophetic of them) and sung to him, two thousand years before everyone else, these so formidable words that Richard Desjardins wrote in his fine song "Lomer," and which my sparrow himself, if he could, would have no doubt chirped:

Il m'instruisit que Terre est ronde
comme on le croit en Portugal,
que puissance et beauté des nombres
feront se rompre les étoiles.

(He taught me Earth is round
as in Portugal they rapture,
that power and beauty of numbers
will lead the stars to rupture.)

Be Convincing

Waking up on the morning I turned twelve, I decided to sort through my ambitions. Lots of options were open to me. I was hesitating between the occupations of writer, botanist, hermit, and philosopher. I didn't know which side to take. I had saved from certain death a white mouse, who was now returning the favor by lending an attentive ear to my confidences. I would bring her into my room and confide my hesitations about the future, because she was a being quite rightfully turned toward the future, at ease with modernism. With visible joy she would observe my life in that fabulous era of tube television sets, watches with springs, rotary telephones, record turntables, telegraphs, and door-to-door milkmen. I remained undecided, but I detected in my confidante "an invincible summer," as Camus wrote, a quiet confidence that ended up inspiring me. I would put her back in her cage and go walk in the streets; I would listen with newfound attention to the planetary cablegram of the insects. One day, I had my little brother Benoit believe that oysters lived in the mountains and to catch them, you had to hunker down in a crevice, wait for them to come out of their hole, and pounce on them. Later that summer, when we were on vacation in the country with our family, Benoit suggested we climb the path to the white cross planted at the summit of Mount Saint-Raymond and bring some oysters back to Mother for supper. It was at that moment that I knew with certainty that I was going to be a writer. In this profession, one must know how to be convincing.

A Donkey

It happened on the farm where I had been hired as a gofer. An old donkey who resided there had latched on to me—I'm not quite sure why—and resolved to follow me everywhere. He would come find me at daybreak, when I dished out the hay. Oblique rays of sun would filter through the barn rafters to touch his long, mobile ears. Later he would accompany me to the henhouse, where I collected the eggs. Next we would snooze in the straw for an hour, side by side, amid the best layers and their clucking. Quite often, I would confide in him about the girl I was in love with but didn't dare approach. His ears would swivel, undoubtedly to capture the Hertzian waves my heart was emitting that year. It was the summer I turned fourteen, I was waiting for something (but what?), I knew nothing about myself or my life to come, but I was grateful for the semblance of destiny I could sense forming little by little in the slightest of my gestures. Above all, I was happy to count among my friends this attentive and cautious animal, still one of the most powerful presences in my memory. Toward the end of the season, what little strength old age had left him wasn't always enough for him to maintain the long work of friendship. The fatigue of forty years of sociological observations, data evaluations, expectation, and devotion to his masters was overcoming the resilience of his once-vigorous body. I don't know if things have changed, but farmers in those days did not nourish their animals with any great feelings. Still, I was given permission to use a piece of land behind the stable, where I rolled a big flat rock to serve as a gravestone for my comrade. I made a habit of going there each morning to pay my respects before dishing out the hay. In a way, I was reestablishing the dialogue interrupted by death. I understood that another reality set in once the last handful of earth was scattered over those thin flanks. It was, it seems to me, the reality of the imperishable memory left in my life by this being who came from I don't know where as if to teach me what human presence is incapable of teaching me, and which might well be the true definition of happiness.

A Crow

I had been the kind of young man who was interested in all the theories, but at this point I was closing my books and casting my gaze far away. The long string of my work, my successes and my tragedies, my luck, my happiness, my disappointments and my constructions to come, and my destiny itself, all that was a blinding line on the horizon. Squinting into the distance, I was still trying to make out the details of that destiny when a crow slipped his way in. I took this great weary traveler, landed at my door to rest, into my home. I gave him something to drink and some excellent food to eat, which inclined him to stay awhile and build atop our spruce a sizable structure to serve as his nest. His presence soon became indispensable to me. He must have been around ten years old, but was curiously ignorant about life. You would have thought he had done nothing but fly over this vast world, without ever touching down, and without ever measuring himself against it. I had to teach him that will is a material force akin to steam, and that its extreme condensation allows for the recovery of a latent energy, subtle, but capable

of shifting the bounds of chance. At first glance, I'd say many of his thoughts had never left his body. But, under the new influence my life was exerting on his, most of them did from then on, in the form of friendly gestures. Often, for example, as I was writing, he would pass by the window time after time, crowing for me to come keep him company. So out I would go, and we would spend long whiles together, me explaining the whims of politics, him marvelously listening while casting me these little sideways glances. I loved what had sprouted without blooming in that mind, pure buds biding their time in the shade. I thought I sensed a humble, kind of sated sorrow in him, but I could see as the light traversed his gaze that his memory was not the natural seat of his sadness. At night, I would picture him in his big nest of twigs, observing the infinite space, the ordered structure of the sky perhaps letting him believe in a mathematical god, poring over his book of equations, on top of his work. Other times he would come perch on my shoulder, and if I pressed my ear to his breast, I thought I could hear inside the measured breath of a young dog sleeping soundly at the bedroom door. He was not a specialist in waking dreams. I think mine intrigued him, amused him too, but they couldn't match the aeronautical view of the world and of life that he needed to make sense of reality.

And yet, by virtue of a certain angle, which was always that of friendship, I could observe around his tilted face the atoms of a kind of conscious meditation, their electrons gravitating around the nucleus. Accordingly, the almost constant presence of a dog and a cat by my side would plunge him at times into a potent reverie, which I never really managed to understand. But I did perceive that it was not absolutely necessary for me to know everything in that respect, that secrets were not an obstacle to the company of beings. One day together, we watched summer slowly amble away down the little farm track. No melancholy was entwined in that fare-well. It was as fine a day as could be.

War Wounded

He was a rather tousled fledgling, still quite astonished to even exist. His injured wing, from which several feathers were missing, was keeping him woefully grounded. I put him in my pocket and brought him home, set him down between two books on the shelf in my study, and there I left him to rest. At regular intervals, over I would go to lavish due care and dripfeed him a concoction of milk and crushed seeds before returning to my desk. And I would feel his grand war amputee's gaze falling on me. Time came, and went. I like to think that, as the days passed by, he imbibed the ideas and philosophical postulations imbued in his shelter, his hospital of books. Anyhow his wing wound up healing, but I soon gathered that he was a being of great inexperience quite oblivious to the laws of aerodynamics and the commonest of flight techniques. I decided I would remedy this shortcoming. Each day I would place him in the hollow of my palm as if it were the end of a springboard and, with the gentlest of nudges, project him all of twelve inches skyward. But he was a contemplator, as they say, whose mind had little sway on the concrete of life. Every attempt would end the same way: as if carrying lead for ballast, not knowing what to do with his wings or his courage, he would plummet like a stone to crash-land on the floorboards, a stranger in his tiny body. And so I would pick him up and put him back in his haven of books, where without a twitch he would spend yet another day watching me write my novel. That whole summer he accompanied me on my strolls in the forest, pitter-pattering his way along the trail behind me. Fall came around. One October morning I found him scanning at length a sky streaked with migratory birds. Then all of a sudden, as if answering some mysterious call, he took to the air awkwardly, looped some perilous loops over the house, and flew off to join the horizon, not without two or three aerial acrobatics, intended or not.

Real Life

It was all happening to me: the electromagnetic charge of success, the dazzling deflation of remorse, the winged heart of the forgotten, the misunderstandings, the betrayals, the white arrow of pain, the barely born blunders that bloomed overnight like desert cacti, humor and its entomologist's eye, a mind lost, found, and dressed up smart again, happiness with its big sacristan's hands. My thinking was not credible, but I compensated by trying to contain the kicking of my young, as-yet untamed soul in the pen of intuition. I would knock at my older brother's bedroom door and ask him to lend me one of his books or another. I dabbled in reading Saint-Exupéry, whose books I could not understand, but whose ample and yet strikingly precise phrases I liked. The words of Albert Camus escaped me also, but there was something familiar in his accents of revolt and nostalgia, in his almost fierce love for the blinding light of the sun. One day, I was struck by a formidable lightning bolt of lucidity. I had just swallowed the last mouthful of my meal when I asked Mother if meat grew on trees. "Of course it doesn't, sweetheart.

It's part of a cow," she said, smoothing back a lock of my hair. Her answer split my world in two. Stupefied, I became an instant vegetarian. I decided to go down to the garden and find Gudule, my pensive albino rabbit. Upon my approach, those long ears twitched to greet me as usual. I opened the door of the hutch and sat down at her level. There I remained for the rest of the day, feeding my little companion carrots and watching the sky turn slowly from blue to green, then from purple to black. Thirty years later I became a writer. I don't know if it's worth mentioning, but every one of the twenty-four books I've written so far features at least one animal who shares the bond of friendship with a child. For a long time after that episode, my mother was worried to see me so uninterested in the play of my own age. But she was growing to know me and took comfort in my interest in gentleness, the pure destiny my tender will was already shaping. I think she was fretting mostly because she knew my quest, like that of the mystics but confined of my own doing to the narrow frame of real life, was a losing battle. On that front, I have changed strangely little.

Peace

When I finished my studies, when I set off on foot and only returned a year later, when my spirit rose for the first time, or when I bid farewell to youth, every time my life has changed direction, I have been struck by an extraordinary sense of peace. I was musing about this the other day when I heard, coming from the forest, the monumental cracking of a tree toppling to the ground. A ten-minute trail walk sufficed for me to find the gigantic oak there, fallen under the weight of its own old age. An owl was perched in a neighboring tree, pensive and peaceful, surveying the scene and hesitant to leave the locale, head swiveling from left to right as if to appraise her chances. On the walk home I thought, in the manner of those who believe in the survival of the soul, that this fine flying being perhaps represented the soul of the giant trunk now lying there on the forest floor. I wondered too if all the beating of wings, the nocturnal calls, and the sudden flights I perceive so clearly in me might be the expression of a similar presence, arboreal and ambulatory, of a peaceful soul appraising its chances of survival for the day I absent myself from my body once and for all.

A Fox

One might think I had a special interest in veterinary care, but I am merely a writer whose curious destiny is to cross paths with creatures abandoned, hurt, lame, or dying. A lot of blood had flowed from the flanks of the red fox who had chosen that evening to come conclude his life beneath our great oak. I did my best, but the bandage I used to patch the wound could no longer stop the mortal from fleeing this body sculpted by will, movement, and a zest for life. It moved me to know that my face, and not that of one of his parents or friends, would be the last image he carried into death. I tried to draw him in to the mysterious kind of dialogue I had fostered with my dog, my cat, one or two horses, and a few cows. But all I could sense was his somewhat febrile meekness, the gentle beating of his heart, and the expression of his gratitude for not having to die alone. I held his paw for an hour, then his eyes closed, something spiritualized in his chest, and after that only the body was left. I went back into the house later and again I reflected that there was no god for the moment, but that it is possible after all for thought or consciousness to be the leaven of a god who rises in the body of people and animals, and who may one day emerge from the matter sublimed, purified if you will. Then I went upstairs and I finished writing the last page of my book, and even though it wasn't planned I put a fox in there with a small role to play. There, that was my day.

Indifference

On Sundays, after eating and drinking his fill, my cat Scooter spends most of the day watching me. The severe gaze cast upon me is that of a merciless judge. If I'm reading his expression right, he wishes I looked more like Humphrey Bogart and could muse as lucidly as Jean-Paul Sartre frequenting the smoky cafés of 1940s Saint-Germain-des-Prés. My lifelong penchant for the abstract and for difficult concepts pleases him none too greatly. He would rather see me defend more assertively the causes I take to heart, and cannot forgive me for having chosen instead as my instrument of warfare the writing of poetic, that is to say, ambiguous, books. He finds my interest in dogs bewildering. He dislikes how submissive they are to their master: to him, this is a form of obedience to fate. The strange joy my life brings me, this silent jubilation that came to me in childhood and each day helps me to live and conquer all, my wonder at nightfall when I see the phosphoric fire of the Milky Way, my speleologist's curiosity about human thought and my constant preoccupation to put my own thoughts in order, my curiosity too about my soul departing me without warning, my saintly intuition every time that, around midnight, the two silent ghosts of my parents pass beneath my window, my ongoing attention to my death, my refusal to think of it as a dead end, my tragic impression of busying myself with things of no interest to most people, my affinity for the telegraphy of birds, for the metaphysical silence of animals, for the green shadows of the forests and the forgotten relationship between Human and the secret matter of the seasons—to all of this he is indifferent. He would rather sleep, and dream the reckless, thrilling adventures of his great feline dream.

Two Ducks

———

For some time last fall I took two young ducks reluctant to fly south together under my wing. The lean-to beneath which this odd couple lived for a month resounded at all hours with a tedious quacking, the result, I trust, of their profound amorous discord. It seemed the female felt affection for her companion the drake, but he wanted none of her affection; what he wanted was for this superb she-mallard to fall head over tail in love with him, as I understood he thought affection was but a bland sentiment, the lukewarm version of love. I found him funny to watch with his heart ringing like a bell and his novice-duck feathers invariably a little ruffled in indignation. He came and went around her with a sway in his step, cursing his fate as a volatile jiltee. I may be mistaken, but I think he was a bird who disliked difficulties because, though the difficulties made him strong, they didn't make him happy, and just looking at him you could tell he was hoping to live happy most of the time, was that so unreasonable? Each day he despaired and lost a little more of his courage when he saw her spending all her time becoming so sage and so conservative, fretting for instance about the prevailing winds or, when I would toss them a scrap of bread, proper table manners. I discerned that he didn't view life as a very serious experience. At his age, he simply had a great appetite for life, if you ask me. He was cultivating the parched plant of his insouciance with some semblance of verve. And yet one could tell from his way of collecting himself sometimes by the pond, by his way too of going about his ablutions, like in Judaism or Islam, that in spiritual life he found real support and felt in his young web-footed body a simple joy, the joy of deepening the sense of purity within himself. In all he was a contradictory being, who lacked seriousness, yes, yet who loved reasoned, cohesive attitudes ballasted by a certain weight. This was especially clear when he approached his darling companion and tried to share with her what seemed to be an overall reflection on the soul of waterfowl. For him she could have been a perky partner with whom to share some debonair pleasures and some difficult ideas but, good God, why did she have to offer him only her lukewarm love?

Body and Thought

However you look at it, a writer's task always remains the same: to describe life as it is, and sometimes in roundabout ways. For a while now, I've enjoyed starting my sentences with these words: "One day, a long time ago..." because they contain my thoughts like milestones. If I were a poet, I would describe the world with a maximum of clarity. More and more, I feel that along with scientists, poets are the best placed to incite people to love life on Earth. But enough said about literature. My Clairefontaine notebook closed, this evening I went to find my dog Camus asleep at the foot of the stairs. I gave him a little shake and invited him to follow me for another of our nocturnal strolls in the surrounding countryside. The moon was casting its pale shadowy light on us. As always, I confided in Camus about various things. I sensed that he was observing me, and that he found my general view perplexing. But all in all, I think he mostly agreed with my inkling that the body is a device for creating thoughts, or emotions (which in essence amounts to the same). I wondered if it ever occurred to him, as it did to me, that, under the pressure exerted by the body, these thoughts may in turn evolve, transform, and refine themselves with time. I wasn't sure, but I was inclined to believe it, since I could clearly see that his powers of deduction, reasoning, demonstration, synthesis, and mute argumentation were shaped at the same rhythm as his aptitudes for running, bouncing, rolling, and tumbling. I was hesitant to go home, to slip beneath the sheets. I figured that tonight once more, something would take advantage of my sleep to drag my soul out of my life and my body. I had nothing against that, but after devoting so many years to building this soul, then to fortifying, expanding, righting, and revamping it, I always feared it would tire of this relentless work and that, when morning came, it would flee from me forever. Good grief, what would my body be without a soul? But perhaps, after all, the soul serves no purpose. Perhaps it is simply a branch of the mind, just a little less dimly lit, that's all. On that, I clearly understood that Camus completely disagreed.

Rainy Night

One night after American literature class, in my rust bucket of a car, I placed my hand on hers. She removed it and said softly to me: "JF, I like you a lot, truly I do, but when it comes to men, I prefer them quite a bit older than you, and most of all I like them to be Black." For a whole year after that discomfiture I bitterly regretted not being Martin Luther King Jr. or even Nat King Cole, then I more or less came to terms with the fact. Thirty-five years later, the wound of that great heartache has well and truly closed, but every time I touch a Black feminine hand, I find myself gasping for breath for a second or two. Around midnight the other night, when the bottle was positively empty, I asked my friend Dany: "Have you ever been in love with a white woman?" He replied, in his big cavernous voice like a Caribbean coconut: "Oh, but of course. But unlike you, I've never wished, as such, that I could become a person of another color. Even today I think that's an important trait of your personality: you're a faux white guy, a Black man who doesn't know it and unconsciously tries by any means to connect to his true nature. At one time it was by falling madly in love with beautiful Ethiopian women, these days it's by hanging around with great black dogs and old newsworthy Haitian writers." Then he paid the bill (some seventy-five dollars) and had to dash because one of his friends in high places was waiting for him, even at that late hour. A mere moment later, standing in the rain, I felt happy and contented, admiring and proud. I always find my life more interesting when I spend a while with highly intelligent people.

Logic and Destiny

I didn't know it was going to happen like that: I was young, and then the next minute I wasn't. At that time, the sky, because of its so uniformly arranged birds, was of an algebraic softness. It took almost nothing, a beating of wings, and all of a sudden I heard my youth push open the little spring-loaded door to the forest. I hardly had time to turn around and see it vanish amid the trees. Even the dog barely noticed a thing, content-ing himself with opening an eye, only to close it again, eager to resume the thread of his pastoral dream. To wrap my head around this suddenness I reminded myself that, in the novel I was in the midst of writing, everything was not necessarily subject to logic. All the more so in life, I told myself. Then, perhaps because my time reserve was abruptly dwindling, I turned for a moment to my youthful years. I don't want to go into the details or else I might fall out of favor with many of my readers, but a fair few of my past follies sprang to mind. Fortunately also entwined with these shad-ier times were the schoolboy, the adolescent, and the young adult preparing with grand altruistic gestures to be the mature man who this evening caught a glimpse of I don't know what dawning of his old age to come. Old age, really? Nonetheless I've always had some intuition that I would die young. But time passes and I'm already two-thirds of the way down the road. If this carries on, I'm going to end up drawing my last breath very old and I'll tell myself that for the first time in my life my intuition deceived me. That's what happens when you accumulate the years even slightly. Over time the intuition of the beginning changes on contact with people, with the light of day, with the rain, with the wind, with animals, with plants, with certain objects. And so Life takes the upper hand and ends up rectifying the destiny you thought was tailor-made for you.

Behind the Shed

I had discovered him two days earlier behind the shed. The young animal showed no trace of injury, but wore on his face the signs of a great lassitude, which allowed me to believe that he had died of some sort of existential crisis, or an immense incurable affliction. Each day his companion came and loitered around the remains, his gaze lost in thought. Not that he seemed despondent, rather he was simply absorbed in rapt reflection, seeking through this conscious contemplation to comprehend something that clearly escaped him. He was not an extraordinary being, there was nothing in his behavior to suggest he had accomplished grandiose things, but to see him so resolutely steadfast, so courageous in the face of pain and woe, you might think he wasn't especially afraid of his own death, perhaps because he'd had the wonderful fortune to have in his life as a porcupine another porcupine who understood him and who, in his own way, loved him with all his heart and all his spirit, and that was enough to fill his life. Frankly, I see no other explanation.

Inner Life

Walking back yesterday along the little dirt track, I stopped by my old neighbor's place secluded deep in these woods. As always, I found his conversation illuminating, and his thinking, put to work for his inner life, extraordinarily lacking in artifice. You could tell he had suffered, but had countered that suffering with a senseless softness. Within him there lay a soul saved from the waters and dragged back by a great flood. His dog, betwixt and between sleep and my company, came and went from the table to the modest rug that served as a bed. A pale light percolated through the windowpane and permeated the furniture. His poems were beautiful. His way of writing them, and reading them to me, made me think once more about Guillaume Apollinaire, whose art was founded on no theory but on an altogether quite simple principle that the act of creating should rely almost completely on intuition and imagination, without ever straying from life and nature. At one point, he said this to me: "I'm getting old, and still I've been inconceivably happy today." Then, at another point: "How lucky, how

lucky I am to have all this time left to live!" Given his age, it was an utterance that took me aback a little in the moment. But on the way home I figured that some people, though well and truly out of childhood, must hold on to the wondrous sense of time stretching to near infinity from that chapter of their lives. Word on the grapevine was, he was a little loopy—and, frankly, I would find it hard to argue against that—but what I gathered was that above all there was too much life in him for a single body. His parched mind bore no hallmark of wisdom, though I did spot side by side some specimens of passionate sentiment, lucid and turbulent thought, planetary and persistently poetic prose. Almost nothing ever happened to him. His sole actions were those of a man minding the potatoes growing in his garden, or counting a few familiar stars at night, or reading a book on the veranda, or even tossing a bit of bread to the ducks in the pond. By way of those motions you could see his soul appearing at the surface of his body, poking up like a plant through the folds of a geological formation. By dint of observing him, I had noticed that practically everything else in his life was not incidental; rather it seemed to obey the movements of that soul. One day, I tried my hand at writing a book with him as the hero. Then I gave up because, as I often do, I found myself colliding with my writerly scheming, my age-old temptation to give sentences shapes they didn't need, to dress pages nonetheless destined to remain bare. Still, the immensely touching thought of depicting men and women simply drawing on their strength, confronted by their dreams and driven by the sole command of their inner life continues to haunt me. In any case, his final words that day were prophetically clear. They were those of a man endlessly moved by love, without which, he murmured to me in the end while caressing his dog, life is nothing.

Kinship

In the middle of last night, responding perhaps to another of his secret intuitions, my dog Camus insisted on waking me to accompany him into the forest. I acquiesced to his request, knowing he wouldn't let me go back to sleep anyway. The little oil lamp illuminated the path rather feebly, but I didn't think what Camus was looking for would call for that much light. I let him guide me. His intimate knowledge of these woods enabled him to advance rapidly toward his goal. It should not have surprised me that a being who had always held such an interest in mind games would possess that kind of mental map. What's more, that mind of his had been his master far more than I had. This he was proving to me again that night as he adeptly ignored my directions, my suggestions, my points of view. Twenty minutes of this excursion amid the shadows sufficed for my companion to lead us where he had to be. A deer, struck by some force or another, lay there before us. You could tell from the heat still emanating from the flesh that death had crossed his path mere minutes earlier. I saw my dog collect his thoughts beside this inanimate body as if standing before a grave. Not a breath stirred the air. All around, the forest was completely silent. A little time passed. Then Camus emerged from his peculiar meditation, looked at me with a pained gentleness of sorts, and, setting off down the trail in the opposite direction, led the way home.

First Steps

When I was thirteen years old, the prettiest girl in school proclaimed her love for me and asked me if I'd go steady with her. My reaction to this drama was to develop a high fever that kept me in bed for days. And when the fever abruptly broke I developed other concerning symptoms. I was in the midst of a mystical crisis and began to believe in the impossible. With my friends, I was having language troubles that led me to construct strange tortuous sentences and unintended paraphrases. My encounters with dogs, habitually simple and engaging, complicated themselves to the point that they began to avoid me. In parallel to these events I found myself acting with an extraordinary courtesy and set my mind to becoming the most endearing boy in the neighborhood, something which rather bowled my parents over. Then I set about repeatedly lifting all sorts of overly heavy objects in order to tone my muscles, albeit in vain, since I was born and I will die with the overarching constitution of a weakling. I dived too with the fury of a sunset into reading *The Brothers Karamazov*, which I would soon however abandon for I had trouble understanding the Russian soul. This lasted some three weeks or so, at the end of which I laid eyes again on the young person who had triggered these rather radical transformations in me. I was nervously initiating a conversation about the weather when, all of a sudden, I found myself slammed against the school wall and impetuously kissed. I then saw my body duplicate and its likeness rise above me, turn for a second to bid me farewell, and dissolve forevermore, like a dream. I stood rooted to the spot, struck by awe and wonder, trying on for size from head to toe this startling foray into the world of love. Right then, two dogs walking on the opposite sidewalk crossed the street with a wag of the tail to hop, skip, and jump with joy around me, barking at the top of their voices. Such were my first steps beyond childhood.

During Death

I don't want to make a song and dance about it, but I died once before. Only, my body didn't remain prone for long; I soon saw it get up and set foot on the little dirt track furrowed in the depths of my life. It's only a detail, but the sky was blue over the pond and the bees were bringing their pollen provisions to the fore. I was walking slowly, as if my old habit of lagging behind was holding strong, even in my death. I was happy because I was learning that what I had suspected was true, that beauty prevailed even beyond the reasonable limits of reflection. My thoughts turned to Albert Camus, dead at forty-six with his manuscript on the back seat, and I wondered whether the book I too was writing before passing would now make me a literary legend. Then I laughed at my folly; the sky was a little off-kilter from the sun's axis and I found this was something far more interesting to ponder. All my life I had been preparing to die, but that day I regretted not having shined my shoes brighter and combed my hair more carefully, the way you do when you have a meeting more important than the others. I had the curious feeling of revisiting the very first moments of my life, when I was about to meet my parents, my brothers, and my sister for the first time. And nevertheless I knew that during my death no one was expecting me, and it was fantastic to feel so free from all hope and concern, to now count on nothing more than the stirring sound of leaves the heart makes as it turns over. I watched the cows grazing in the fields as if trying to find the right words inside themselves. At one point, a fox passed by and regarded me as if he knew me, and I recalled our erstwhile encounter, his injured paw, his ailing and already so strangely light body, my unavailing aid and his last breath in my arms. It surprised me to find death altogether so lively, not succeeding life, as we always see it, but standing back to back with it, so to speak. It's only a detail, but the birds were fluttering from one branch to the next and the sun was shining like never before.

Enigmatic Questions

My first extended contact with animals, at the age of five, left me in awe. The same sense of perfect surprise captivated me a year later, when I went on my first elevator ride in Montreal. Who and where was the driver elevating my young body this way? It's curious, the rapport I've had, since then, with animals. Every time I find myself in their presence I seek out those cables, those shock absorbers, those pulleys, those doors that open and close again, those speed limiters and counterweights I can sense moving in my body at any given time. Often, when I'm done scratching my head over those questions, I quiver at the thought that animals might cease to understand me, or simply amble away from my life. For that matter, a lasting unease, spurred by a sharp shock to my psyche, instilled itself in me one day when, out in the field, a Starbuck-sired bull to whom I had taken to reading Mallarmé's anti-realist poems suddenly rejected me and backed away toward the herd. And so I went home with the idea in my head of a universe filled with enigmatic questions. This twist of mind remains lasting. It lingers among the few ruins that since the end of childhood have scattered their old stones among the foundations of my life. What I would like, what I'm waiting for, is a way to more directly enter the animal world, which, it seems to me, is more multidimensional than we believe, more interested in intellectual life than it appears. "Whatever am I going to do with you?" my mother would say.

Imagination

I've never had a lot of imagination. I consider that all the books I've written are just pieces of remodeled reality. It's perhaps because I lack imagination that I write every day (from eight o'clock to noon, more or less), in hopes that over time the ideas will come to me, at least a little way. But most of the time great thoughts run away from me, and that's why my books are always so full of practical objects and down-to-earth considerations. I try of course to make these objects more literary by applying a sort of science to them but, no, all in all I don't think I have much aptitude for concepts, only an irresistible attraction to a certain tangible beauty: the moon over the pond, the oh-so-mysteriously peaceable deer, the extreme timidity of the four-toed salamander who lives in my garden, that sort of thing. To prove it, you'd have to conduct two or three laboratory tests on my body, but in my opinion the few creator's atoms in this body serve me far better to rectify the real than to remake it. It occurred to me recently that when I was writing a book I imagined nothing, dreamed of nothing, but that I leaned with all my weight on the somber, uncertain, complex, open, flexible, and changing truth of my flesh and my existence, and that I was seeking thereby a way not to transform my life but to push it a little further.

Sleepless Night

Late in fall around here, let's say in the last days of October, a murmur in the air that masked the rustling of the leaves over the summer gives way to the organic, woodsy sound of the earth. Last night, Camus was grappling once more with one of his bouts of insomnia. That's what happens when you spend your days reflecting on the problems of our time. As always, at his request I got out of bed and took him out to stretch his legs beneath the trees. The great bare ghosts were creaking a little from the cold and from their sap flowing slower than in the halcyon days. But most of all it was the sound of something way farther above that intrigued my dog. I reckon that if he turned his ear, he was listening for the return of that distinctive swishing of the stars against the sky. It must have been around three o'clock when I suggested we go home, and he refused. I left him to his meditation and returned alone to go back to sleep. Pulling back the curtain this morning, I saw him right where I left him (at the foot of the old oak), eyes closed and ears pricked, the way you listen to a piece of music that moves you more than the others.

Root Cellar

———

Over time, the notes gathered in this book end up resembling a newspaper left open on the table you come back to at the end of the day when the dog has had the longest of walks and at last has no further need of his master, when the garden is weeded and the house is neat and tidy. I amass in it certain things I don't know what to do with, most of the time of no importance, but which an uneasy sort of hunch urges me to conserve. From childhood I've carried this stubborn fear of falling short of ideas and especially words to express them. At eight years old, I heard that women's ovaries only had a limited reserve of eggs. I don't know why for a whole year after I learned this startling news I had it in my head that the brain too contained but a limited number of words and ideas. That was the dumbest and dullest year of my life: I was saving my words and my thoughts, I wanted to stretch them out at least until I turned fourteen. That bean-counting preoccupation of mine has since largely eased. But something of it remains. Hence the provisions of words here and there, stockpiled like potatoes and cabbages in a root cellar.

Hence, also, my secret alliance with animals, and my penchant for the roundabout route they take when communicating with humans.

Whistling Bird

My body believes it is still young, until I instruct it to behave like it did fifteen or twenty years ago. Then I find it more hesitant, less inclined to deploy the frankly rather imprudent sort of determination in which it used to specialize. When I question my body, the answers I get are no longer as clear as before. I can see my comrade slipping away, the one I could count on no matter what, and in his place I'm beginning to discern a distracted, or daydreaming, presence, occupied with something other than my life, and which deprives me of my solitude without keeping me company. Now I try more or less successfully to stand with my back against the doorframe of this mind of mine. I do my best to redress my ideas and my great useful obsessions, but more and more this body coerces them into a curve I had not foreseen. Fortunately, I'm coming around quite well to the idea of these new shadows taking shape on the horizon. Of course they don't make things any easier, but to me aging is not that much of an inconvenience: I accept that I'll be entering this age where thoughts, sensations, and feelings can almost live by themselves and dispense, some days, with their physical medium. I can't complain: all in all, except for its two or three betrayals, which for that matter set me back a lot, I've been able to count on this body that is so full of indefinable strength and ill-thought-out gentleness, and I've been well served by its natural attraction to invisible things. I continue to live as calmly as possible, hands in my pockets, eyes fixed on the door that stands ajar, over there, right at the far end. In the bare branches of a neighboring tree whistles a little winter bird.

What Would
I Have Been?

On a farm I visited in a dream last night, an old horse spoke to me: "What would I have been? I don't know how to say it other than by harkening to the peaceful, wise foal I once was and who continues to live in my body, and the fire that sparked early in my mind, and the hours where the water lilies of memory and the finite pastures of the future are now melding. Yes, what would I have been? Each day, this human society beside which I have lived, utilitarian, militarian, American and Catholic, obsessed by entertainment and technology, kills me a little more. All the gods people have invented for themselves bore me. The beliefs in a paradisiacal world succeeding this one amuse me for a brief moment, then exasperate me. Fortunately, I can still discern in myself a kind of poetry I believe is a thought being born, and I also sense this impetus, honestly quite mysterious, where with no sensible explanation I start to believe in those days when I was happier than I sought to be. Nothing has erased itself either from those moments when I advanced in certain dreams as in love (with the impossibility of turning back), thanks to which today I find comfort in life, and each morning when I open my eyes something in my thinking agrees with life. Yet I have suffered greatly, my masters have mistreated me, and once I very nearly died from the blows; I lay a week long almost bled dry in the straw. I shall not forget the little bird who each day would fly into the village to open the automatic doors of the mini-mart, peck at the exposed fruit on the shelves, and bring enough back in his tiny beak for me to survive until the next day. But, above all, I remember the dear mare who helped me take my first steps away from my death and who, when at long last I made it to the window of the barn, murmured in my ear with a dizzying tenderness: 'There you are. You're back at long last.'"

The Modern World

I'm rather fond of the past and its great objects endlessly encased in the encaustic of memory, but in no
way does that mean I take no interest in the modern
world. On the contrary, each passing day seems to me
a little more inclined toward a radiant future than the
last, with its such admirable complexity, its extraordinary inventions, its web of unifying thoughts, its
science and its schools little by little rectifying foolishness and hardship, its serene memories, its pleasing
atheism. Only, for a reason I cannot quite fathom, I
remain somewhat in the back seat of modernism. Perhaps deep down this body that carries me and in which
my orbital soul swirls is that of a man destined to be
late, lagging behind the times with his old straw hat
on his head and his overflowing watering can, filled
straight from the rainwater barrel, in hand. It's just a
vague memory, but I think I recall there being a border
of flowers in Mother's belly when I was in there, which
I would go weed whenever I could. By contrast, I precisely remember that it was in this place that I heard
for the first time, resounding from the other side of my
life, the joyful barking of a big dog who was waiting

for me. I quite sincerely suspect that it was from that day onward that I began to stray from my era and the passage of time in general in order to devote myself to nothing but the reverence of animals and the cultivation of plants and trees. Later, long after my birth, I naturally added to these pursuits those of the fine writerly craft, but I don't believe I have achieved in my books the degree of perfection I perceive in the eyes of a cow, a horse, or a fox, or even in the delicate lines of a lily's stamens.

Comma

———

Today I devoted the entire morning to the editing of a text only to delete a mere comma. Around noon I pulled on my boots, my heavy coat, my mittens, and my beaver hat, and the dog and I then set out to follow the snowy trail to the mountaintop. Up there, an eagle drew giant circles in the icy air, dropping great meteors on us with his eyes. Later I made a fire in the snow and Camus stretched out so close that steam rose up from his damp fur. While I was waiting for his nap to be over, I pulled out of my pocket and reread the old second-hand book I love so much because it opens by itself right at the·page its previous owner read so often. A half hour passed before we went back down toward the house. At one point, I don't know why, it occurred to me that at this stage in my life in order to keep on living I would need not to be helped, nor to be more loved, but rather to be supported. From time to time in the distance we saw timid little creatures running away, hares or stoats, which the dog, squinting, didn't even bother chasing. Then the house appeared between the bare branches. At almost that very moment Manon came home from work, so the three of us went and snuggled together before the hearth, and my thoughts turned to those who don't recognize the face of their happiness. After dinner I sat down again at my desk, returned to the place in the text where I had deleted the comma, and reinstated it. Such is a typical day in a writer's life.

Poetry

Shortly before sunrise, Scooter came to drag me from slumber with his great five-toed paw. I followed him downstairs, where he insisted I sit by his side on the shabby old sofa. An hour passed during which he only stopped meowing when I read him one or another of the poems in René Guy Cadou's fine volume *Poésie la vie entière*:

Toute ma vie pour te comprendre et pour t'aimer
Comme on se couche à la renverse dans les blés
En essayant de retrouver dans le silence
L'alphabet maladroit d'un vieux livre d'enfance

(All my life to understand you and love you
As we lie on our backs amid the corn
Striving in the silence to revive
The clumsy alphabet of an old childhood book)

As he listened to me, in his green gaze I recognized his everlasting enjoyment of difficult books, the kind that pose complex questions and interrupt our usual manner of conceiving of things for several hours or several days. The theories of the German philosopher Arthur Schopenhauer, inspired by those of Plato, Kant, and especially the sacred Indian texts, still move him considerably, albeit less so than during the time of his life when we first found him in a cardboard box and adopted him to chase mice. These things said, that morning I sensed he was more drawn to ideas of a simple matter, requiring no tension of mind. To see, I set aside Cadou's poems and began to read him the Gospel of Luke, in my view the most interesting of the four by reason of its spirituality saturated still so little by religion. But no sooner had I begun than he resumed his meows of protest, since Scooter is not a cat of great faith. As ever, he would rather rely on his capable instincts to perceive the very moment when subatomic matter transforms into thoughts, dreams, love, or courage. Memories, too, he finds particularly moving. How many times have I happened upon him, staring into space, revisiting in his mind the pure moments of his flown-away youth?

Le soleil va paraître
Déjà les souvenirs entrent par la fenêtre

(The sun will come out
Already the memories are coming in the window)

Trees

When I have ceased to be in this body, if possible I would like to become a tree. The ideal would be to shelter season upon season various families of crows, or occasionally a couple of owls, but I have nothing against the idea of homing a solitary squirrel as a permanent resident. The one I see every day in the poplar branches seems to me to possess the personality of a literary being, in other words who ventures out little, who dreams conscientiously, who has their own inkling of beauty, and who is always more or less attuned to the sounds of the world, but without the molecular concentration of a scientist. It's just an assumption, but I think what he's secretly hoping to find, by staying separate from society, is a part of his lost happiness. This I dare say because even when he's taking a nibble of one or another of the countless nuts in his stockpile, he always seems absorbed in some sort of retrospective reflection, as if dwelling on a wound of old, an old coal fire left smoldering. When I was young, not far from our house there was a field with a mildly electrified fence to keep the cows contained. Sometimes I would touch it without meaning to, and feel my soul pulsate with a little seismic trepidation, like the frisson of love. It would be folly to suggest that trees can feel this, but they may well be a receptacle for these charges of affectionate electricity, which would explain why so many creatures go and nurse their sorrows among those branches.

Woe Is Me

———

At home, my brothers, my sister, and I lived by the sense that each of us was connected to the others and that if one of our bonds were to break, we would all collapse. The glue that bound us together was not a thing of principle, of morals, or of convenience; it was something rather more cheerful. For instance, whenever one of us was unhappy, worried, or bedridden by fever, or by contrast happier than usual, the others would huddle around and set about cracking jokes, playing pranks, and getting up to all sorts of hijinks. In this family of little tearaways and outlaws, laughter was one of the finest ways for us to love one another. Sometimes, because life was too big for me, I would get up early and go bombard them with questions. But dawn did not suit the dusky spirits of my siblings, who loved to sleep in. And so I would leave them to their slumber and their snoring, only to pounce on them as soon as they were out of bed. Good grief, when someone sets their mind to it, they can be a real pain in the neck for a whole bunch of others! Then I grew up. I'm not saying I have more answers to my burning questions than before, just that things seem simpler to me now. I think I could live without working much, without overly dreaming, without sleeping much even, and eating nothing each day but a hunk of bread. Oh, but if I were to stop studying, searching, and analyzing, especially if I were to interrupt my exploration of the metaphysics of animals, and to cease listening to the dulcet voice of their god digging his great hands into the container of the earth, yes, if I were to stop all that, then, woe is me, I would be lost!

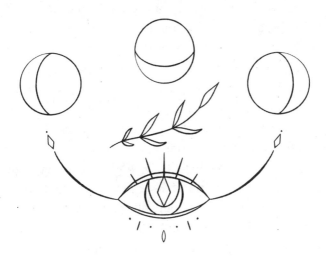

God's Journal

Today I died. On the narrow trail leading out of my life I saw birds I recognized by their plumage, creatures on their way to drink, and a great many pollinating insects. Farther along I ran into the writer Jean-François Beauchemin climbing the slope, heading home in the company of his dog Camus. Now and then there came the stirring sound of a cattle farm and, resounding from the little lake, the splash of the water when Jesus dived off the dock. Halfway there, I recalled my surprise when I peered over Isaac Newton's shoulder and read those so-unexpected equations of his, then my astonishment on discovering the content of those of Albert Einstein. My shock, too, when I began to take an interest in the work of Marie Curie on polonium and radium, and the revolutionary findings of Louis Pasteur. Three hours of chemistry and physics thus sufficed to undermine my faith, and four drove me to atheism. It is perhaps not easy to grasp how God can come to cease believing in himself, but being understood is no longer what really matters to me now. Now that my presence is no longer felt and the human brain is relieved of its need for the absolute, as it were, I would like for something new to spark in people's minds, for people to begin to love the elementary simplicity of their spiritual lives for what it is, to stop quaking with fear before the shadows, and to find interest for all the right reasons in the idea of infinity, so enigmatic, so harrowing, and so tumultuous, charged with a centrifugal joy, bestowed with a great magnetic force, and, no matter what people say, so profoundly connected to this earthly existence.

Winter 1975

It was a delicate and almost fatal, but altogether successful operation. When he woke an hour later, and after many a cold sweat on the veterinarian's part, my cat however was no longer the same; gone was the one he had been for so long, whose thunderous presence in the house had etched itself into memory. New ceremonials ousted the old. He grew into the habit of roaming around places where he used to be miserable. My theory is, he wasn't drawn to misery as such, but rather he was seeking a point of comparison between his pleasures lost and those he was now encountering. What was the god so dissatisfied with its work to the point of starting over from scratch, taking this feline in hand and transforming him into a suddenly so jovial and flourishing being? This lasting state of plenitude, satisfaction, and serenity, which he lived in an admirable balance of mind and body, extended as far as his interactions with me. By degrees I saw him become of an amiability I had not thought possible in this temperament that was once so caustic, so scathing in criticism. I would observe him contemplating the night sky, where he seemed to have finally found what he had earnestly sought. It was as if, in the midst of the star-studded night, his life were illuminated, as if the trajectory of the great celestial bodies circling in their orbit were helping it to take its own measure, to establish its order of magnitude in this organized system. At noon, lifting his head once more to the heavens, he would calculate the angular height of the sun above the horizon, pore over the comings and goings in his inner atlas, reproducing the poignant camber of it all with a set square in the logbook of his body. I adapted my existence to this model, striving to rectify if need be the relative position, the movements, the structure, and the evolution of my destiny. At times, I would envy the strength contained in the tenderness of my little companion, and I would rely on this to toughen the resistance of my poor freshwater crustacean's shell. Wide winter clouds passed over the house. Together we listened as the coughing spells of the wind rattled the windowpane. Later the calm returned, the moon ascended among the clouds. Its interest in us lost, the storm had fled.

What There Is in My Memory

"In every human heart there is sorrow," my mother would always say. She was a woman of practical mind, but nonetheless vested with a great faith, which is to say that she believed in certain things she knew to be false. Sometimes I had to translate her silences. The finest of them would beckon me into vast speculative reflection. She would sometimes try her hand at writing but, whenever she put elbow to table, nothing but a few wandering wasps made it onto the page. She knew foolishness was a tough beast to tame but she kept faith, since she saw by observing her children that reflection is a practice one can acquire. But she also knew how to dream, and when evening came she would tend an ear to the roof and listen to the rolling of waves and the swash of a sky swaying amid its great astral figures. The love she gave us took a great weight off our shoulders. What she loved most of all was to see us playing rowdily in the yard or in the street, healthy, free, sound of mind, and understanding. She was happy to live in a time when such marvels occurred. Strictly speaking she was not solitary, and yet the dreams she dreamed at night almost always depicted a life led away from other people, as if her body had adopted the wrong mind and ended up with that of an owl. You would not say she was a serene sort of person; I'm almost certain even that in the end her heart was broken, but at least she tried something. Her personality inspired me, her soul moved me, but her example has never enticed me, and this is surely why I believe I have not been frightened or defeated by my life. And nevertheless, like her, to make headway I must almost always go beyond my strength. I often think of her death as a small and little-frequented train station, stranded in a suburb of the light.

A Supreme Discretion

It was as if he were dreaming of invisibility: to see all, hear all, learn all, with not a palpable thing to signal his presence. He was a dog who very much loved life and people, and manifested this but did not want to leave a trace. He was neither shy nor troubled, neither unhappy nor afraid; simply, he took interest in the activity of the mind, put into practice his particular inclinations for frugality, nurtured a pride in life that prepared him for the future. I often figured that if I could have infiltrated his soul, I would no doubt have found myself in a vast waiting room. I didn't really know what he was waiting for, but in any case I noticed he was doing it with some kind of organic captivation, some primal force hinging on the use of a fossil radiation far predating the current cosmological period. In many aspects, the two of us lived twin lives together, each leaning on the other and barely separated by a common wall. One day, I pulled on my big boots, grabbed my shovel, and went with him to clear the snow blanketing my parents' grave. When at last I saw the modest inscription on marble again, I recalled as I caught my breath that when I was young my mother would marvel at the extraordinary silence surrounding me. Turning to my dog, I then wondered whether or not, a bit like a sniffer dog detects certain objects buried beneath debris, he had uncovered in me the vestiges of that childhood of silence and supreme discretion, only to reproduce them in his own life.

Vocabulary

One day, one of my teachers closed my exercise book, handed it back, and said to me: "Before writing a novel, you must acquire some vocabulary." On the way home from school I got it into my head that a good way to acquire vocabulary would be to immerse myself in the pages of dictionaries. At the dinner table that evening, my parents were thrilled and genuinely astounded to hear me say I wanted to receive all twenty red volumes in the *Encyclopedia of Youth* series for Christmas. The winter of 1969 was consecrated to this soporific reading. In June, on the brink of depression, I shut volume four with a definitive snap, then out I bolted from my room to go climb trees in the nearby forest, wander the banks of the frog stream, and build the fort with my friend François that would serve as our headquarters in the fratricidal war against the snotty little brats from the west side. My modest vocabulary grew considerably richer over the course of that pitched battle against the enemy. It developed ever further on connecting with my friend, with the girl next door I found so pretty, and with my parents whom I interrogated incessantly about genuses of trees, families of birds, and species of frogs. Literature is never far away from the real world.

Everyday Life

I don't believe my cat Scooter holds much space at all for religion in his life, but certain ways he behaves give me the impression all the same that he feels he is a part of a great divine whole. This he experiences especially, I think, when the contingencies of current affairs confound him, when turns of events around the house, evading his intelligence, oblige him to make use of his other faculties. Then I see him, moved by the functional poetry of a rain trickling down the gutter, absorbed by a moral system mysteriously devoid of rationality, seeking in other animals the company of amorous admirers, the many misunderstood, and those who marvel at minutiae on the pettiest of pretexts. In his worst moments, I find him quite the proselyte, scouring the village and recruiting disciples here, there, and everywhere who'll do anything to follow him. And yet, no, I'm almost certain that religion plays no role in that little, lithe, purring body of his, propelled by a heart of gold. This is just a hypothesis, but could it be that God is manifesting in Scooter, and that Scooter is conscious of this, but it seems insufficiently significant to him to make a song and dance of it? As if God had been knocking at the door in his absence, and the mere traces of his visit were enough for him.

Four Dogs

At a certain time I shared in the life of four dogs. Boomer was promised a bright future but behaved in the mean-time like Francis of Assisi, whose dissipated youth had suffered the spoils of mischief and tomorrowless amo-rous conquests. Einstein was a specialist in shoplifting, forcing us once a year to hold a garage sale to liquidate the stolen goods unclaimed by neighbors. Bozo had a thing for culture, particularly the kind in my library, where he would quite literally devour books, assimi-lating his knowledge by way of the digestive tract. The last, Oslo, was introverted and geographical: he would wander off incessantly, not for lack of discipline, but for the love of travel. From his odysseys in the surrounding streets he would bring back mental images to replay in a loop, his young pheromone-packed brain functioning almost exclusively on the same principle as these mod-ern devices that will repeat a selected snippet with the push of a button. This discreet, humble companion so disinclined toward social interactions was also, per-haps all the more because of his qualities, the scapegoat of our little canine clique. "For the best conductor is lost in a bad orchestra." (Franz Werfel)

Spring

———

Dawn was barely tinting the sky when I left the house with the dog. Most of the birds were still sleeping and their perceptible minuscule musings were hovering pensively over their nests. Perhaps because for some time I had been going through a sort of spring of the mind, I told myself at that precise moment, and without knowing from what part of myself this sentiment came to me, that the finest years of my life were those I had not yet lived. Following which Camus ran past me and tore off along the trail, as if his youth were all at once warming his paws, or his soul were suddenly in a hurry to live. I felt singularly free from worry, but the thought that so many well-meaning people were unable to change the course of things was engulfing my life with an impatience of sorts entangled with sorrow. In the words of Simone Weil: "All that is highest in human life, every effort of thought, every effort of love, has a corrosive action on the established order." Then we walked awhile beneath the trees, and once again I felt an undecipherable joy irrigating this great body I have inhabited for such little time, it seems to me, but from which I would still have to resolve myself to separating. Next I was absorbed in contemplation of a woodpecker clutching the trunk of the ash that has been growing for fifteen years beside the pond. For a quarter of an hour, this curious bird pecked away the bark, casting uneasy glances all around, like a nervous mechanic under the hood of a car. Later still, as I stood skimming stones across the water's surface, I recalled how one day I had quite in spite of myself had to turn my life on its head. Three days long I cried, but once my body was well and truly emptied of tears, at last it could then fill with ambition, and so surprising forces then began to support me. I wouldn't go so far as to say that I started to believe in God, but what would I have become without the assistance of what does not exist? In my opinion, we have a desperate need to lie to ourselves, and especially when reality falters, because reality only rings true if we invent a beauty for it. Then the dog and I went home and all day long I wrote various things and did a few chores in the garden. It was soon going to be that time of the day when the sun pours its big bucket of gold over the countryside and commences, in the west, its slow slide down the mountainside. All around the house little squadrons of birds were traversing the air at low altitude, as if to breathe in the scent of mown grass more freely. Around seven o'clock I turned off the engine of the mower and went down to the far end of the yard to collect my thoughts by the grave of my dog who died some years ago. The modest mound of stones stood with its back to the void; the little annex of the garden arranged for the humble sepulchre remained in a way the capital of my sorrow. As always, at that time of day when everything seems possible, I called out, as I used to call to feel the rub of a snout against my leg, or the love of an aged animal already tired of living but still happy to walk beside her master. Her ghost came to me, emerging softly from the forest, a scarf knotted carelessly around her neck by one or another of her new masters in death. True to our tradition we stayed a long while not making the slightest sound, this dog of mine contenting herself to lick my face and my hands, me to caress her mighty chest where the rhythm of life continued to beat, but more allusively, as if in memory. I was happy to know she was now in the shelter of time, cocking her ear for distant news from Syria and North Korea and their ballistic missiles, or for the deep and elusive voice of eternity. I was relieved that her arthritic and rheumatic suffering had now visibly ceased. Then she returned to the forest with a tranquil kind of assurance, stripped of all regret, and when I saw her long red tail altogether disappear into the thicket, I went to put the mower away in the shed. Another admirable day was drawing to a close, sated with practical work and abstract considerations.

Faith in the Future

One day in the month of May, I saved from drowning
a coyote pup who had ventured a little too close to the
rapids down at L'Anse aux Vigneault cove. I still twitch
at the sentiment of feral gratitude expressed toward me
by the pup's mother. A month or so later, I was sitting at
my desk, making the finishing touches to a paragraph
when I heard from afar the long vesperal howl typical
of these wild canines. The moon was high above the
treetops when I stepped out of the house, collar turned
up, and ventured into the forest to answer their call. A
light wind was shifting the arrangement of the atoms
around the trees. A few clear stars accompanied me,
slid by the sky along its wide stellar avenues. At the
rendezvous point I recognized the mother coyote lying
on her side, heinously hurt, bleeding to death. The little clearing where I spent the next few hours watching
over her remained sparsely lit, one or two big clouds
veiling the moon in a modesty of sorts. From time to
time I whispered a word or two of encouragement to she
who was dying. I like to think that she was leaning on
those words as she aspired, in the middle of that night
so full of the absolute, to assimilate the weightless,

dimensionless, timeless shadows that awaited her and that she could surely already sense emerging from within. The wind had calmed. The flowers were closed. The world stood still in startling immobility. Yet one thing subsisted. Perhaps because she was thinking of her pup back in the den, I could sense flickering in the mind of my coyote the fire of some kind of faith in the future. The creature, however, never saw the sunrise and died with the last of the stars. I made my way home, escorted by a few silent birds.

Glory

Once, because I had written a book they liked, some people in very high places pinned a medal to my chest. Then I was invited by them to some very grand parties, during which I was asked to speak about all manner of things. I graciously gave in to their demands, but I knew any number of them had far more interesting opinions than mine. Later still other people rewarded me once more and once more they wanted to know what I had to say on this subject or that, and I answered their questions, I was kept very busy, I had become an object of curiosity of sorts. This went on for a while, then I grew tired of it. I began to turn down the invitations and the honors. I found that my garden, that domestic life, that the comings and goings of the birds in the feeder and the changing color of the sky were more captivating. Perhaps I lacked ambition, but I discovered that I had no need for so much attention, recognition, money. Then, one day, a young child who came to visit told me he thought the animals I doodled in my notebooks were funny. I don't know why, but his minuscule, limpid laugh, escaping through the wide-open windows of my house, made me happier than all the public recognition of which I had been the object thus far. True triumphs are discreet.

Wing

This is another story about an injured bird. Today a hummingbird crashed into the window and fell crumpling and stunned to the deck below. I scooped the little body up and administered the requisite first aid. Then I made my little protégé comfortable in the fork drawer in the big china cabinet, and several hours of a fabulous convalescence commenced. An unspoken closeness settled in between us. I found the courage to open up to him about the causes and effects of a recent heartache. As I confided in him, I adjusted the dressing that now covered his shoulder. Still, it seemed he was suffering less from his crumpled wing than from the solitude into which this forced stopover at my place had plunged him. I stayed close to home and tried to reassure him of my intentions. Only he feared me not, or little, he was a creature who seemed not to have been born to worry but rather to feel the pain of loss, separation from loved ones, and also the suffering of others, which visibly distressed and outraged him. On the other hand, I could see there existed in him a real happiness of mind, soul, and body, a need to incessantly consider and, one way or another, construe its raison d'être. I tried to probe him further, but admittedly this was not an easy subject to get into. By four o'clock, the miniature mechanics of the wing were working again. At the time of his release, two of his acolytes, little aerial sentinels, no doubt keeping watch there since the accident, flew out of the potentilla bush and came to escort the patient away.

Beauty, Patience

As a young child, whenever I planted a seed I would unearth it every day to see if it was growing or not. When evening came, lying in bed, stiff as a board, I would command my big brother Pierre to come measure the length of my body. Had I grown at last? A deep despair would descend on me as soon as I heard the answer I so detested: "Not by a whisker." I would then give my brother leave to return to his debonair dreams. The following day, rising early, I would stand at the window and implore the sun to hasten its pace. I would open the newspaper and consult my horoscope to see whether I could expedite access to a future I imagined tailor-made for me, filled with dogs, forests, and agrarian undertakings. Then, one day, my mother and father came home from the hospital with a new baby. After dinner when I was allowed to hold that tiny hand in mine, I distinctly heard a door slowly opening in my mind. It was the door of patience. Some time passed. I observed the newcomer living. Weeks, sometimes months would go by before this fragile little thing learned something new, and yet I was filled with calm and a kind of irrepressible joy. In the end, the newcomer became my little brother Jean-Luc. This is the great lesson of my life: what is truly beautiful is the work of time.

Fleeting Friendship

This dog was lost, or abandoned, without a tag and without the slightest grievance against the human race. I questioned that Buddhist gaze, imprinted with an incomprehensible calm, translating a familiar thought with both despair and the highest peace. Various interferences prevented me from communicating with him as easefully as I would have hoped. I was tempted to call on my friend Kamal, who claimed to be able to converse with dogs in the Bantu language of his African homeland. Then I turned to other solutions more within my reach. I figured such a spirit must love fine literature. I absented myself for a few minutes at a time, long enough to pluck two or three classics for him from the bookshelf in the little room down the hall. His sighs told me the rather heavy rhetoric of Victor Hugo was not pleasing to him. Claudel's devout Christianity made him fearful, and sent him hurriedly seeking refuge beneath the table. By contrast he very much enjoyed the extraordinary perfection of Baudelaire's verse and the hallucinatory youthfulness of Rimbaud, which brought us a considerable closeness. He was a nostalgic, that much was clear from the way he sniffed at my collection of old objects and so completely ignored the few modern devices scattered throughout the house. I am hesitant to compare my mind to that of a nine- or ten-year-old Labrador, but I think that if he and I shared the same interest in the past, it was mostly because all told the past is a present that has survived in memory. I was tempted to adopt him. I had seen two other dogs live in our house (not counting Camus, barely out of puppyhood yet) and I had learned from them what a fine, accomplished existence was. I reflected on the life we could live together, in this kind of intellectual zeal unique to those who enlighten by their rapport with nature and people. I nevertheless began to put the word out in the village about the presence of this fine lost animal in my home. I secretly hoped his owner would not come forward. That was not the case, and three days later I had to say my goodbyes to my companion. We parted with regret, he holding out his big blond paw to me, and I wishing him a long and lazy old age.

Manuscript

Yesterday, my publisher traveled nearly a hundred miles and came to the house to pore over the manuscript for my next novel with me. The usual flaws were quickly detected, highlighted with a Staedtler pen, and then the conversation forked toward other topics. Somewhat melancholically, we touched on the life of the poet Claude Gauvreau (dead before forty-six) and his so impressive way of writing, tending toward the unknown. Then we talked about other writers, and about the country existence we each lead, him beneath the fine clear sky of the Appalachian plain, and me atop one of the least populated of the Laurentian summits. During this time Camus persuaded himself of his strength, thinking he could twist our arm by standing staunchly at the door and staring at the handle. But we resisted his requests, which immersed him once more in his natural state of concerned introspection. To claim this dog is bestowed with a soul might be overstating it, but still we sensed in him the manifestation of a solar action, a spirituality of the forest—yes, the presence of a waning sun, the faded glow of a being faced with a tougher reality than others. In the end, my visitor retrieved from the fridge the smoked salmon he had brought with him and cut it into thin slices, which we drizzled with a little olive oil and lemon juice and then wolfed down with a healthy serving of arugula and a generous glass of chardonnay. I think I can safely say that once I've worked on my manuscript for two or three days and fixed the dangerous pitch of its rafters, I'll be done with this occupation of mine for at least two months. I'll make the most of the opportunity to properly plan out the vegetable garden, repaint the deck, plant yet more trees, and pay closer attention as well to this dog of mine, who has been giving me looks full of reproach for quite some time.

In the Field

Not far from the family home there was a big field where pensive cows grazed, their minds on other things as they chewed the cud. I had formed quite the friendship with one of them and had taken to visiting her every day, as she seemed to like me reading to her. Around three o'clock, seeing me approach with my book, she would nonchalantly wander away from the herd and meet me under the oak tree. I may be wrong, but in my opinion she was an intellectual who was particularly enamored by sentences that were brimming with striking adjectives. We would while away the time together, I reading to her out loud, she daydreaming as always, a tuft of grass in her cheek, swiping the flies away with her tail. Then I would hear Mother calling me for dinner. I would bid my companion farewell, crawl under the old fence, and whistle my way home, my dog-eared book in my pocket. One day, my cow vanished. I never saw her again, not in the field among her kind, and not in the barn. When I think back to this, I tell myself that perhaps she ended up becoming a character in the farmyard fable of her mind, and that all our literary rendezvous gave her food for thought.

Strolling

This morning I rose early and went for a walk in the countryside. With a zig and a zag, the dog led the way down trails still running with the rain of the recent days. After a half hour or so I sensed something pass through me that was neither a memory, nor an idea, nor even a shiver or intuition, and so I figured it was decidedly not necessary to believe in God to have a divine feeling. Then, not far overhead, as if skirting the sky, birds began to flutter from tree to tree with little feverish exclamations. We imagined they were in search of an abode in which to raise their nestlings, or at the very least a place to rest, or reflect awhile, for instance about the unspeakable Syrian war and all those poor people dead for nothing, now standing in the hereafter, a bouquet of flowers in hand. Later I found my dog suddenly rather systematic and reflective, as if all his experience on Earth were abruptly deploying its power in his big blond body. It made me happy to think of him growing old by my side, bit by bit becoming the dog he had hoped to become, as well as to think of walking in his company toward the not so faraway traffic circle where human tenderness and animal sensibility converge. Next I wondered why, in my pragmatic human mind, one in four thoughts were inhabited by the insight that animals have an inner life at least as fiery as that of humans. Finally I reflected on my luck, especially that of living the last thirty years with a woman so created that in order to understand her, I must not think, but dream.

Dizzy

I asked my dog to wait for me in his kennel, I got on my bike, and I rode like a madman all the way to the village. I then sat patiently in a chair until I was called, whenceupon I sprang to my feet and almost sprinted out of the waiting room into the doctor's office, and no sooner was the door closed behind me than I nervously said: "Doctor, I must be sick, I only feel well when I get dizzy." He had me take a seat, leaned down over me, and pressed his stethoscope to my heart with a frown. Then he drew himself upright, gave his big bushy mustache a pensive rub, and proffered this advice: "Walk right out of here and fall in love. For what is love for, other than responding to a need for dizziness?"

Where Dreams Begin

Two days ago, coming back from a walk along the path beside the stream, I encountered Jesus once more. This has often happened to me in the course of my life, but today like yesterday my dealings with the divine remain distant. Quite quickly though, after the customary greetings, the conversation took a decidedly frank turn. "Is your conscience at peace?" he asked me, in his strong Hebrew accent. "At peace, that would be pushing it," I replied, trying to get to the bottom of the so-enticing mystery in his eyes. He was not beautiful to speak of, but he made me think of those people, of whom there happen to be many, who are only beautiful because of the decisions they make and the thoughts that condition those decisions. Next I spoke to him about some of my faux pas, about two or three heartaches I caused and that haunt me still. I was hesitant to say more, but in essence it was not very hard for me to admit the errors of my ways as I could sense that I had within me what it would take to repair them. Then he wanted to speak again, only I interrupted to ask a question of him: "Do you sometimes feel that you're missing something?" He replied that of course, there remained some significant shortcomings in himself, but that one day he had decided once and for all to be thankful for what he had been granted, instead of lamenting what he had been refused. I found this to be an interesting answer, albeit difficult to apply. Following a short silence I further asked: "Where do you think the dreams I have at night come from?" And so he observed with an affected fascination the gentle swaying of the treetops in the breeze, then he appeared to concentrate intently on the song of a black bird whose contrasting yellow feet gave the comical impression of wearing boots. Then, intrigued, he bent down and, pointing to a little flower with white, reddish-striped petals, asked me: "What's the name of this plant?" I told him it was wood sorrel, which could be found across Quebec, at least as far up as the fiftieth parallel. Then, as if to himself, pensive as ever, he whispered these scintillating words: "Take a good look around you. This is where you begin your dreams." You could see by the way he had survived the cross that he believed in life, and loved it, which, in my very personal view, I opined, was by far the finest of beliefs. We took a few more steps together. I noted that his sandals were unevenly worn, undoubtedly by reason of his innumerable comings and goings amid the unaccommodating rocks of the

Judean Desert, between Bethlehem and the Dead Sea. "Why were you so set on becoming a writer?" he pondered at one point. "Hmm," I replied, gathering my thoughts as best I could. "I don't really know. Perhaps to have at my disposal as pure a time as possible, devoid of all serious work."

Purity

On the day of my birth, besides my mother of course, and my father with his hat and wrinkled old raincoat, one of the first living beings I encountered was a bird. Mother had insisted on leaving the open cage containing her Waterslager canary in the bedroom. From the bottom of my crib I listened to the little songbird, whose repertoire was limited but always infused with grave subtlety, with whimsy, with reserve, and with excess. An outline of intimacy was traced between us. Because my young mind had not yet molded to the human language, this made it all the easier for me to shape the brittle clay and translate the song of my canary into intelligible terms. His first words addressed to me, dare I say, were to warn me against grief, followed closely by a few recommendations concerning love. He lingered at greater length on this second subject since one must always, in his opinion, take greater care to talk about tenderness than trouble, which contents itself with the first words that come. In any case, that was what he taught me, and this is why in the books I went on to write unhappy people are most often described in a, let's say, detached kind of way, whereas those whose happiness is apparent always seem to wear a sort of monarchic crown on their heads. To get back to my canary, he would repeat over and over to me that he was born to find something, but that he had forgotten along the way what it was. I watched him live, and made a note of everything in my memory: his perplexity, his trials and errors, his vacillations, but also his jubilations, his passions, and the tireless battering of his shoulder against the jammed door of the future. Mother let him be ludicrously free, but that freedom was never more than a base, a pedestal. It was up to him to find a way to erect a monument, some sort of construction on which he could lean in the future. I learned from him, during the volcanic months that followed my birth, to become the sculptor or architect of my own life. This will seem curious to read, but in the end, I mean when in some decades' time I hear in the driveway the discreet but decided step of my death, I think that most of the things I will have experienced in my existence will no longer really matter. Only, I would like to remember those first contacts with my irreplaceable bird. Yes, when I hear my death stopping on the other side of the door and calling me with its inexplicable voice, I would like to see him again in spirit and hear him say to me, if possible: "It may only have lasted as long as a song, not that it really matters. Those few months together back there, in that little bedroom, were they not of a wondrous purity?"

A Woodpecker

By dint of being a writer, I've come to understand that there are always words to say it all, even when it comes to the most difficult of things to describe (death, or time, or even some extreme forms that beauty takes on). I've realized that when words haven't come to me, it hasn't been that I've lacked vocabulary, it's that I've lacked poetry. To talk about things, you have to notice them. What does poetry do? It illuminates the part of the world relegated to the shadows by the senses and by ordinary reason. It's a lighting designer for the stage of hidden realities. In my manuscripts, when I've had enough of writing as if I were lining up jars on a shelf, I try to offer my mind other perspectives than that of my Cartesian pages and slip here and there between the lines the odd troublemaker, such as a word borrowed from a discipline other than literature. This is not only beautifying but also adds an alluvial layer to the ensemble, a sight that might spur literary archeologists of the future to make two or three interesting discoveries. I wondered whether the woodpecker who had been coming every morning that month to proclaim his bachelorhood by hammering at the gutter was resorting to the same ruse. Yet twenty-one days of that hullabaloo had led to nothing but a falling-out with the squirrel who was nesting close by. But I noticed that in the fourth week his pecking became more harmonious, or let's say less cacophonous, allowing a refrain to ring through which sounded, I imagine, quite close to an ornithological kind of poetry. Perhaps it's just a coincidence, but anyhow I have to add that a female woodpecker eventually came along to the gutter and the newly formed couple promptly took off arm in arm, if I may say so.

Joie de Vivre

One day, our neighbors Mr. and Mrs. Chung, whose house clings spectacularly to the mountainside, procured a goat mostly by reason of the capacity these animals have to hold their balance on steep terrain. With spikes on my shoes, every day I would go sit by her side as she grazed on one or another of the sagebrush-studded slopes. She ignored me supremely, but I was insistent in my approach to try and pierce this kind of mind that had so fascinated Pablo Picasso, that he said contained the very essence of joie de vivre. This goat was not what one might call a being of action. Rather she specialized in the contemplation of landscapes, in the ingestion of domestic plants, in the flicking of a tail, and in the occasional caper. The words I addressed to her were tender and precise, as any words must be that seek to capture the secret pleasure of living, the reasons for being of joy. What surprised me was that her joy seemed to necessitate only a negligible amount of effort, as if it were natural for her to be happy, and unhappiness only ever materialized in her in the form of a pure ghost, a fleeting and fleeing shadow. I'm not sure if I should say so, but sometimes I step outside my body. Oh, but it's not an esoteric operation that opens up an immaterial dimension of my self! I simply dislodge myself from my life and take a few steps back from myself for an hour or two. I distance myself from the man I am and with whom I find myself tending more and more often to dis-agree. I watch him sap his strength, exhausted by the thousand contradictions of his age, contending with his briefest of human adventures. I know he won't always manage to get away with unlikely coincidences like the one that once saved him from a certain death. But what I like best is to see him daydreaming. His dreams are truer than his life, more ravaged and more painful, more prone to danger and more combative, more sub-versive and more functional, more sure of themselves. I'm surprised he has so poorly understood that, even once he's exhausted those images, his curiosity will keep inventing new ones. I explained those things to Mr. and Mrs. Chung's goat. But she, as always, was only con-cerned with her joy and her solitude, with her selective weeding and her four stomachs.

A Hare

He was a solitary hare who lived in a hole in the middle of the forest, in the compact shadow of the great larch. I would see him almost every day when I passed right by his place, the dull thud of my footsteps driving him to peek his perpetually astonished little head out of his den. One day I found him not far from there, caught in a snare, exhausted, and frankly in quite a bad way. One knee to the ground, I cut the wire that had been choking him slowly but surely for at least an hour. Death came nevertheless. The grave I dug with my hands was soon covered over, then I went home. Three days went by during which I worked more studiously than usual on writing my novel. One evening, as I was watering the garden, I sensed a presence behind me. There was my hare, his neck still bearing the marks of his injuries, his long aerodynamic ears pointing to the sky. "I've been asked a lot," he said, "what was there in death, where I lingered awhile, long enough to acquaint myself with it. I found it complicated to explain that there was nothing, no objects nor images, no memories nor thoughts, no feelings nor conscience, no God, nor creatures, nor any person. But the most difficult still is to say without passing for a fool that I nevertheless brought back from my stay the imperishable conviction that my life is not meaningless, and that in order to bring it to fruition I must listen, keenly observe, connect with strangers, reflect and marvel, not be disheartened, and persist when everything seems to resist me. It's not that something is waiting for me at the end of it all, because there's nothing. But I do think that between now and then, my little contribution is required."

In the Garden

Today I rose at dawn with the firm intention of writing nothing all day. A light, barely mobile mist hovered over the garden. For an hour, the dog and I walked amid the plants, the stones, and the subtle song of the earliest birds, immersing ourselves in this almost immaterial cloud. At the center of the circle of old blackened stones, the embers of last night's fire in the pit were still smoking. Next the cat came and joined us, still wet and weighty from his nocturnal hunting. Then, around six o'clock, the mist lifted, and it was as if a curtain were opening and the actors in the play were warming up on the stage. The birds were suddenly no longer subtle at all, and the whole place started to stir with their atmospheric melodies. A mere moment later the air began to move, and the leaves and the flowers too began to flutter. In the sky something shifted, and the whole mechanism controlling the turning of night into day creaked a little, like a pulley. Over the house, three or four sparrows escorted a paling, departing dream. Some minutes later, her soft face still cradled in the cushion of sleep, I saw Manon appear at the window and wave to me with a smile. It was all tremendously beautiful.

Sources

APOLLINAIRE

The calligram "Mon Cœur pareil à une flamme renversée" (My Heart like an inverted flame) referenced on page 36 was excerpted from Guillaume Apollinaire's collection of poetry *Calligrammes: Poèmes de la paix et de la guerre 1913–1916* (Calligrams: Poems of Peace and War 1913-1916), published in 1918 by Mercure de France. (Translator's note: A calligram is a visual arrangement of words used to represent the content and meaning of the text. This calligram and other examples can be found on the Allen Ginsberg Project website at allenginsberg.org/2014/07/expansive-poetics-86-apollinaires-calligrammes.)

A HOUSE SPARROW

The lyrics of Quebec singer-songwriter Richard Desjardins cited in French on page 39 are excerpted from his song "Lomer," from his 1998 album *Boom Boom*, produced by the Foukinic record label and published by Editorial Avenue. (Translator's note: The English lyrics provided are my own free translation.)

BE CONVINCING

The few words of Albert Camus quoted on page 40 are excerpted from his essays *L'Été* (Summer), first published in 1954 by Gallimard. English translation excerpted from *Lyrical and Critical Essays*, edited by Philip Thody and translated by Ellen Conroy Kennedy, Vintage, 2012.

POETRY

The two excerpts of poems by René Guy Cadou on pages 94 and 95 are from his collection *Poésie la vie entière*, published by Seghers in 2001. (Translator's note: The English versions provided for ease of reading are my own free translations.)

FOUR DOGS

The Franz Werfel quote on page 112 is excerpted from his book *Le passé ressuscité*, first published in 1928 and sourced here from the 1992 Livre de poche edition. The English translation referenced here was excerpted from *Class Reunion*, translated by Whittaker Chambers and published by Simon & Schuster in 1929.

SPRING

The Simone Weil quote on page 113 was sourced from *Œuvres complètes, t. II: Écrits historiques et politiques, vol. 1* (Gallimard, 1988), first published in 1958 by Gallimard as *Oppression et liberté*. The English version referenced here is from *Oppression and Liberty*, translated by Arthur Wills and John Petrie, first published in 1958 by Routledge & Kegan Paul, sourced here from the edition published by the Taylor & Francis e-Library, 2004.

About the Author

Two-time Governor General's Award nominee Jean-François Beauchemin is a prolific French Canadian author whose novels, poems, essays, and contemplations have earned great critical acclaim. His work has been called "one of the best-kept secrets" of Quebec literature. Among the more than twenty published titles to his name, only one has previously been published in English (*Turkana Boy*, Talonbooks, 2012, translated by Jessica Moore).

After graduating with a degree in French Studies from the Université de Montréal, Beauchemin worked for many years as an editor, copywriter, and radio producer for CBC/Radio-Canada. His first novel, *Comme enfant je suis cuit*, was published in 1998. But it was only after releasing four further titles, including *Garage Molinari*, which was a finalist for the 1999 Prix France-Québec, that his work began to attract wider attention. His 2004 novel *Le Jour des corneilles* won two prestigious international awards in 2005, was shortlisted for the Prix des cinq continents de la francophonie, and went on to be adapted as an animated film, released in 2012.

ARCHIVES OF JOY

A sudden and serious illness in 2004 that left him in a coma for days, on the brink of death, led Beauchemin to devote his time entirely to writing and probe the depths of this profoundly life-changing experience in a literary trilogy spanning four years, from 2006 to 2009, and blurring the lines between fiction and nonfiction. The author describes his writing as a "way of remembering." His books, each in their own way, delve into the human soul, marvel at the mind and the senses, and celebrate the beauty in the world.